To Susan

A JOURNEY TO CAMATKARA

Best wishes

Synn Kune
2013

by

SYNN KUNE LOH

ALPHA GLYPH PUBLICATIONS

Cover Design: James K-M
Cover Painting: *The Tipping Point* by Synn Kune Loh
24"x24" acrylic on canvas, 2012

www.SynnKuneLoh.com

Library and Archives Canada Cataloguing in Publication

Loh, Synn Kune, 1947-
    A journey to Camatkara / by Synn Kune Loh.

Poems.
ISBN 978-0-9781705-4-7

    I. Title.

PS8623.O43J68 2012   C811'.6   C2012-903269-7

For Dawn:
your mother's name is Hope,
are you the chance hope brings?

For Catherine:
love invents us.

Prologue

The Birth of Great Happiness

The night is finally quiet,
but my heart is far from still. .
I listen for the silence
that will take me beyond
a poet's eloquence.

I stand in the corridor of time,
and you are but one thought away.
Touch me gently while I sleep,
to brush away the boundary of dreams.

We are new moon to all the stars,
violet lightning opens the midnight sky.
This is the night in which time begins.
Stand with me while I hold your hand.
We await in great eagerness,
the birth of a new consciousness.

The foundation has been shaken.
We awake to celebrate

the birth of great happiness.

PART ONE

CAMATKARA

ECSTATIC WONDER

o

o

o

A thing of beauty is a joy forever.

- John Keats -

POETRY

Words exist because of meaning.

Once you find the meaning,

words fade away

Where can I find the poet

who has found the meaning

to write the poetry

I have not heard?

PAINTINGS

A painting is more than a thousand words.

I am the painter

who has forgotten the words.

Look at my paintings.

Can you see what I forgot?

A Dialogue on Luminosity

Suspended in time's covenant

unread vision restores

an ancient rhyme.

A scent of immortality

stirs the beat of the soul.

Eternal Resonance

The luminous charm of quiet laughter

echoes through time.

The warm glow of souls' silent whispers

a beam that shines.

Angelic Presence

It shines from the inside out

An image

a motion

a thought

echo of the purest sound

reflections of the

purest thought

DELIGHT

Where do colors come from?
The change of season catches one unaware.

A look into the depth

of the soul.

A tingling recognition of wisdom,

so old.

Quantum Entanglement

Let fall reality

the unheard

the unseen

now echoes

Inward to the Heart

All the treasures are locked inside a cave.

Sunlight on water

moonlight on ice

each reflection

bringing us closer

to our purpose

ZOOM LENSES

A map of unnoticeables

solar wind

crystal emotions

electric time

blue thoughts

radiant soul light

quiet anticipation

distant footsteps

warm kisses

sweet embraces

cool dreams

Discovery

The mind moves with a complex precision

Who was the man

walking by the sea?

All the sunlight

falls on his shadow.

ABSENCE AND PRESENCE

A delicate intuition that is undefinable

Who was the woman

looking for love?

Ready to embrace

the next smile that comes her way.

ASSUMPTION

A realist never sees miracles

Who was the girl

coming from Oaxaca?

She could heal him

with a touch of her hand.

Solitary Tale

The sky is never empty

the earth is always full

Who was the child

reaching for a star?

Coming back with

the book of life.

GRACE

Standing on the threshold of eternity

Clouds roll away

boundless sky

holds my spirit

in close embrace

CELEBRATION

Predisposed response to beauty

Spring rain

calls me to life

random thoughts

deeply transparent

a sigh of forgiveness

unfolds the beauty

INFLAMED PASSION

Here is your desire
and you didn't even know

Summer days are long,

mountains beautiful.

Crickets sing in the ravine

lavender flowers cover the meadows.

The raspberry season is here.

My joy bursts into bloom,

by a smile of the goddess moon.

CHERISHED STORIES

Regardless of the reasons

Early autumn

temple stands tall

bare and ancient.

On the steps,

leaves fallen,

ten thousand stories

in folded silence.

THE DANCE OF SIVA

For whom do the flowers grow?

Open heart

open mind

plum blossoms' scent

strives in deep snow

Earth Calling

What fulfills an inner longing

Mountain storm

had let up

Winter retreated

earth preserved

A double rainbow

framed the road

From behind temple doors,

golden faced buddhas

take a peek at the world.

PART TWO

IN THE EYES
OF THE CHILD

o

o

o

MY SPECIAL FRIEND

Scene One

The child stood

at the edge of the star field.

He was always the same age.

He was my friend.

We spoke in shimmering lights

and emerald visions.

Two thoughts,

through time

and space.

My Special Friend

Scene Two

Relentless search

burning shadows

molten gold

an ancient echo

The quickening of crystal tones

the heartbeat of the universe

What world is this?

What life is this?

Spaceships moving out

Exodus to a big red sun.

My Special Friend

Scene three

Beyond the moon

beyond the planets

my friend waits

walking the star field ...

collecting starry fragments

and placing them

into my dreams

CONTACT

Early morning

darkest hour

indigo light

crystal columns

Silver angel came to greet me

with stories of fallen giants.

A ball of white light

fell into my hands.

The room burst into

a shower of radiance.

I sat up alone in my bed.

Five years old.

FASCINATION

The eye loves novelty

Someone quietly quietly

taught me

to smile

into city sounds.

One by one,

butterflies of different colors

came out of

concrete high rises

to light up the sky.

Anticipation

In the not too distant future

The new gate is open

At the end of the year,

I will be one year older.

I can go to the garden,

but not old enough yet

to walk alone in the woods.

Happiness

Sitting on the edge of contentment

On a ferry

I leaned

outside the window,

and let my spirit

be swayed

by the passing wind.

Trembling Delight

How to watch the sky

The clouds carry many tales.

Catch one,

put it into your pocket.

Share it with me,

at the next full moon.

PROFOUNDLY MEANINGFUL

Invisible but for their songs

In the garden,

among flowers,

I saw once again

angels and stars.

In the hour of dreams,

I will look for them

to remind me,

"God's children

are never alone."

PLEASURE

Lavish and luscious

Eating ice cream

on a hot sunny day.

I was warm all over.

Should I hold it in my hands?

It would melt my longing.

ESCAPE

There is no such state as absence

The western sky

deep orange and violet

No one knew

I had slipped out of the house.

I went to the garden.

Gathering rain,

my shadow walked into the pond

taking with me

cherry fragrance

and evening dusk.

Sweet Comfort

Then comes a breath of air
enough to unsettle a leaf

When I was small

I wanted the constellations

to stand in line,

waiting for my command

to start the dance.

Now I am glad

they are still in their rightful places,

so I can find them

when I am a guest

in someone else's home.

A Sense of the Mysterious

A special privilege

A smile came

through the moonlight.

Angels returned

to my heart's delight.

I would dream

to leave the earth,

to climb the Milky Way,

to follow the sun's path.

THE CALLING

Inside life
Outside time

In the classroom,

a decision was made.

I must go to the forest soon,

before all the colors

leave the woods.

INTERLUDE AT A STREET CORNER

Light flowed from my room
to the market place.
Past was losing its memory
to a future unknown.

I stood on the street corner,
waiting for my ride to school.

Buses, trucks, cars, people hurried by.

Somewhere in the city,
a house was burning.

Somewhere in the city,
anger ruled the streets.

Outside the City Hall,
a preacher was selling his truth.

In the market place,
a child asked, "Mother, what just happened?"

Out of the corner of my eyes,
a blue globe came rolling down the street.

I wanted to be in the game,
not just an observer on the street corner.

But I was only nine.
I didn't know how
to enter and exit the many hallways of life,

I could not slow the traffic,
or help the man in the gutter.

A wall of sound came crashing down
onto the pavement.

The hollow heart of the city
cranked up its volumes.

The city was talking loud.

The street was moving fast.

Brand new condos called for tenants.

The clock on the tower struck nine.
I had missed my ride.

I turned to follow the blue globe.
brushing away the lies that flooded the news counters.

I must go home to find something
to help me to remember.

The Beauty Way

Life thinks of itself in me

The blue sky
fills the wingspan of a bird.

The world
fills the eyes of a child.

The mountain
fills the echoes of the ages.

The sea
fills the depth of longing.

My heart in love
embraces the universe.

My heart at peace
stills the wind.

There I sit,
under a tree.

The child dreams.

A Wish for Tomorrow

Something discovered yesterday

Come out of your quiet room.

In your body,
a decision is made.

In your mind,
a hundred questions.

In your heart,
a thousand longings.

In your soul,
a call goes out ...

I want to leave home.

My birthday wish,
fourteen years old.

PART THREE

FAMILY TALES

o

o

o

The other page of truth

Family Tale 1

In the beginning ...

I was two ounces five in Chinese esoteric calculation.

The fortune teller shook her head, "This boy is not destined to stay home."

Grandmother took it hard, "But he is the first born in his generation. There are expectations and responsibilities. Look again."

"His constitution with nature is winter fire. It does not burn by itself. He needs help from outside the family. Let him find his way in the world. There will be others who will help him."

Grandmother pleaded, "How long do I have him?"

"Eighteen and no more."

"Are you sure? Check again."

"The story has already been written."

FAMILY TALE 2

There are times
in which the world is empty

We had a big house in Guangzhou, I was told. Everything was lost soon after my birth.

Was I to blame? I wondered. A first born son was supposed to bring good fortune.

The family escaped to Hong Kong. The new house was much smaller.

I felt trapped, a child growing up in an adult's world. So many people all the time.

So many voices. Gossip was like thunder.

Family Tale 3

To come to know the world,
I must leave myself behind.
Here I will not call on the sun,
but endure the shadows,
and overcome my fear of it.

I listened to the voices of the night.

The house was breathing, taking in all the sleepy wanderers.

My cousin stirred in the bed next to me. My aunt snored gently on
the far side of the room.

Outside our door, my uncles stretched their weary limbs.

Upstairs, grandmother and others walked through their dreams.

I could see unseen beings in those days. An earth guardian stood
by the entrance. My spirit friends came to greet me, bringing gifts
from the four directions.

Then I wished they would stay with me, that the experience would
remain familiar, that I would always have a safe haven, reconciling
one dimension to the other.

However, all that would be forgotten soon.

FAMILY TALE 4

The restraints of life,
a retreat into deep still water.
In faith and hope
a whole life altered.

I was five years old, asking for my mother. My birthday was coming.

I thought she would be there.

No one said anything. Surely, a child's faith could move a mountain.

I kept the secret to myself, my birthday surprise to everyone.

Many years later, I saw the photograph. There was a birthday party.

I had a hat on with the brim turned around, blowing out five
candles. My face was sweet and innocent.

Over time, I thought I had gotten over the disappointment.

My mother did not come. Not that year, nor all the years after.

FAMILY TALE 5

You are more valuable to me
than you think.
I had a glimpse
of all that is yet to come.

Grandmother kept me from trying out for the basketball team.

Her explanation: the fortune teller. My destiny was to be a scholar and not an athlete.

I got upset and joined a team in the playground.

It was not the same. We had no uniforms.

FAMILY TALE 6

I need more than ever
to find the thread
that holds everything together.

One Sunday, I wanted to go on a picnic with my class.

Grandmother cast an I Ching oracle. It was not favorable.

She forbade me to go out of the house. I was mad.

The next day I returned from school and complained to her, "Everyone went and had a good time, except me. There was no disaster."

She simply said, "Because you did not go."

FAMILY TALE 7

How could one hold back the tide,
the need to explore life?

Amazingly, a simple thing such as a student bus pass gave me my
first taste of freedom.

Good for four trips a day, the conductor punched a hole on the
card for each ride. Some days, I walked to school to save a ride so
that I could explore the city later.

Grandmother knew what was going on, but didn't say anything. I
ignored the worry in her eyes. As long as I made it back home by
six thirty, just before dinner, it was fine. Years later, I realized this
was a test of trust between us. I wish I had known it back then.

My school was on a main thoroughfare. I would choose a bus at
random. My favorites were the double deckers. On the upper level,
I opened the window wide and let the wind rush at my face.

My favorite route was to take the No.2 bus to the end of the line.
Next to the station, a small lane full of night market shops led a
path to the harbor. From there, small ferries took passengers to
places outside of the law. I made friends with a shop owner and
wanted to know more about those places.

She told me one was famous for dog stew, another for gambling,
and then there was one where a little boy like me would be
kidnapped and sold to faraway places in southeast Asia.

That stopped me from going onto those ferries.

FAMILY TALE 8

What we are
we are like no one else
joined together
in a most abundant way

Grandfather lived with us, partially.

He had three wives, two lived under the same roof.

Grandmother three was somewhere out there in the city. She got him for the weekends. She seldom set foot in our house, and was not mentioned in our family except during major festivals. Pillow politics ruled our household.

Grandmother two was sick most of the time, suffering from neglect beyond repair. My grandmother was his first wife. She held the family together.

When grandfather took ill, my grandmother joined with grandmother three to look after him. I believe they actually became friends, from adversaries to allies.

Forgiveness was made through action and not words, something I must remember.

FAMILY TALE 9

In every life lies a journey,
and in every turn
a choice has to be made.
Somehow, we all have to live.

Grandmother's good old days: Yards of silk, gold coins in her
dowry, the number of servants.
Her family: A manufacturer of an aromatic preparation, an all
purpose healing ointment. Big money.
Her marriage: An arranged marriage, an accepted social custom
among wealthy families in those days.

During the war with Japan: A heroine.
Grandfather had to leave town. Grandmother took the family on
a long march and walked from one province to the next to escape
from the invading army.
Most remarkable: She had bound feet in her younger years.

Her character: Kind, resourceful, and caring. She took in all the
relatives who just came out of China. Our home was like a railway
station where every train made a stop.

That is why it had to be painful for her to argue with grandfather
every month over allowances.

Her worry was a burden to us all.

Family Tale 10

Again and again,
pushing the boundary
pointing to the limits
turning into a stranger.

For a long time, Grandmother did not give me any pocket money. Was it an oversight, a life lesson or more nonsense from the fortune teller?

I watched my classmates with envy as they had money to buy treats from vendors who gathered near the school entrance, especially the man who sold a snack called "white sugar cake."

He carried his goodies on a round bamboo tray balanced on his head. A damp cloth was used to keep the cakes moist. The texture was spongy and chewy. The taste had a clean sweetness highlighted with a touch of vinegar.

Students loved the vendors. Teachers and parents hated them. Street food was not hygienic, and these men could be criminal characters. Notices were posted telling us not to buy from them.

They achieved the opposite results. It was not just about buying snacks. It was a social occasion where kids hung out with each other after school.

To belong as one of them, I needed to buy snacks and ate the forbidden food like others.

I don't remember how it happened. I began to steal money from my grandfather's pocket, coins at first, and then dollar bills.

I was caught, but not punished. The look on grandmother's face froze my heart. Grandfather simply gave the instruction that I was to have five dollars a week as my allowance.

His only comment, "If you become the top three in your class, I'll give you more."

It did not work. My grades got worse.

Family Tale 11

Open your eyes
to something greater
wanting to bloom

I did something bad during the last term of primary school.

Our art teacher, Mr. Wong, told grandmother that I had a natural artistic talent. Grandmother rejected the notion.

She said to him, "Art will get him into more trouble. He daydreams his life away as he is. He will become a scholar."

I kicked a chair and tore up two watercolors.

After, I was caught cheating during a history exam. The surprised monitor that day was Mr. Wong.

He stared at me and said, "How could you?"

I was stunned.

My punishment was to get an F in history that term. Grandmother was upset beyond words. I brought shame to the family. From then on, I quit art classes, and tried to avoid the teacher.

Mr. Wong had a nickname, "Coffin Wong," because he looked ill most of the time. There was a Chinese saying to describe a very sick person, "One foot in the coffin." Mr. Wong died during the following term.

The students did not know he had cancer. I was one of the nasty voices cursing him to his coffin.

FAMILY TALE 12

Trust is a commodity
to be handled carefully.
What have I done wrong?

I went to a Jesuit all boys high school. It was a struggle to
be disciplined. Later, I realized that the Jesuits were far from
disciplinarians. The prison was in my mind.

Against all odds, I was chosen to be the head student librarian and
given the authority to purchase books from students' perspective.
It was my first grown up experience.

I was well received at the bookstore. They led me to the
manager's office, and I was served tea. Tired of Hardy and Dickens,
I asked for great writers from Russia, France, Germany, America
and Japan.

The priest looked at my purchases, "You used up several years'
budget. A lot have to be sent back."

I answered, "Books will last forever."

He said, "Are these for you or for the boys?"

I did not answer. He shook his head and walked away. Half the
books were returned.

I was the first and last student head librarian.

Family Tale 13

There is always a place for you
at my table.

In high school, my taste in street food graduated from vendors to food stands in the night market. Naturally, I was forbidden to eat there. The food was not clean; the customers were no gentlemen. However, I found the smell of cooking and the sounds of laughter most tempting. I also got a secret satisfaction from eating in a very uncultured manner. At home and in school, I was reminded about my manners constantly. At the night market, there were no such restrictions. People ate with their mouths full, chewed loudly, and drank soup sloppily. The more noise a person made, the more laughter followed.

After staking out the place for a few weeks, I finally found the money and the courage to sit down by the counter and order a bowl of soup and noodles. First, I cleaned the chopsticks by putting them in the glass of hot tea. Then I slowly tasted the soup and carefully picked up some noodles with the chopsticks.

The owner took the bowl from me and said, "Boy, let me teach you to eat like a man."

He wolfed the noodles down in three gulps, raised his head, licked his lips, made a big sound and pounded his fist on the table. Everyone laughed. I looked at him in awe. At that moment, he was my idol, the most content person in the world. He slapped me on my shoulder. I almost fell off my chair, but my heart was warm all over.

Quickly I learned to fit in. He always had a special soup and noodle for me.

Family Tale 14

There is a poem at the center of your life.
Treat it with calibrated optimism.

In Hong Kong, the antique district was famous. Streets were
narrow with heavy traffic. Cobble stones paved the lanes.
Interesting stores called out to pedestrians.

At the antique booksellers, I loved to listen to their stories about
old manuscripts, rare books and obscure documents. The musty
smell in the stores infused me with a sense of mystery. They let me
read bound copies of first edition treasures.

One day, I wrote a poem in couplet form from my grandmother's
teaching,

"Among books are mansions made of gold,
poetry in your abdomen makes Qi grand."

The owner showed it to others. There were oohs and aahs.

One man commented, "This boy is no ordinary fish in the pond."

Another said, "Go home and listen to your grandmother."

Suddenly, my whole world seemed brighter.

FAMILY TALE 15

Can you see me
a small person
against the wind
against the rain

One day classes were canceled because of typhoon warning. In the
morning, there was only heavy rain. The wind came after lunch.
Number seven signal was announced. The boys were excited. No
more school that day. They rushed to leave.

A strong feeling came over me. My heart was all tangled up. I
stayed behind and watched for a long time until the wind and the
rain became one.

The priest found me in the empty classroom. I told him that I had
no sense of belonging in the world. He sighed and sat down with
me. He told me that he was cut off from his family as well. Ireland
was a mystical past. He got the calling, to serve God and not man;
to be in the world, and not home.

He said, "Some of us are destined to serve in faraway places.
Perhaps you are one as well."

A smile came to me for the first time that day.

I told him the vision I had when I was small, "I will climb the Milky
Way, to follow the sun's path."

He gave me a long look, "An unusual young man with a peculiar
mind. We have to be careful with you."

He sat with me for a long time before asking the driver from
school to take me home.

FAMILY TALE 16

Dispense with the rules
avoid solid ground
search for that precise timing
when you are you

The priest became my mentor. I was sent to do some voluntary work at the Botanical Garden, an oasis in the middle of a concrete jungle. It was hard at first. I was out of my element. I'd rather be at the movies.

My supervisor was both the gardener and the groundskeeper. As we walked through the park, I wanted to learn the names of the flowers and plants. He said names were only names. They meant little. I would learn more by observing.

He gave me a zen riddle one day, "Flowers are not flowers. Flowers are flowers. Who is watching the flowers?"

I laughed at such nonsense. The priest sent me back to listen. I did not pay much attention. I wanted to learn something useful, not idle talk and riddles.

The old man's name was Mr. Lee. He was a restaurant owner. After retirement, he became a volunteer worker at the garden. He loved flowers and plants his whole life, but never had a chance to tend to them, until now.

A week later, as I was picking up garbage from the walkways, Mr. Lee motioned for me to come over, "Do you notice anything?"

"The flowers are blooming," I answered.

"All the flowers," he beamed.

I said, "Is this possible?"

"Normally, no. Every species has its own season."

"How did this happen?"

"I did it. I used mental energy to make an experiment."

This was getting to be unsettling. He continued, "I have the ability to talk to plants and flowers."

"How am I going to report this?" I wondered.

"No, you don't write about flowers. You write about how miracles happen and few people notice them."

On my final day, Mr. Lee said, "Remember the famous saying from Chairman Mao, how he mobilized a revolution?"

"I have no idea," I answered.

"Let the ancient serve the present. All the flowers bloom at once."

Family Tale 17

Come,
let us be guided
by the spirit
of all things

In the Chinese literature class, I wrote an essay, "Confucius was a failure."

My teacher took me aside, "Who gave you these ideas?"

"No one. The facts told the story."

He shook his head, "Do not write this again. You will fail the examination."

I took the essay to the bookseller. He said, "Good boy, but this will get you in trouble."

He took me to the back room among his rare book collection.

"Truth came from the ancients. History was only biased opinions. It is important to know how to find the key."

I asked, "How?"

"Intuition. Some have it, most don't. I leave you here. Choose a book that really matters."

Without looking, I reached out and picked one, It was the Yellow Emperor's Internal Canons, the classic text in Traditional Chinese Medicine.

FAMILY TALE 18

The mind is wild,
wild with the visions
that tame it

Grandmother was worried about my academic performance.

A teacher told her, "He is a smart boy. He can do a lot better."

She cast oracles looking for my success. The answers were all
favorable, but they did not improve my grades.

One day she said to me, "You have no parents to support you. I am
an old woman. The best I can do for you is to give you a ticket to
America, You will have to earn your way through the university.
But first you need better marks to get a scholarship. Stop your
wanderings and study."

My wish had been answered. How little I knew about my
grandmother.

While I thought I was trapped at home forever, she had a plan for
my freedom.

I told the priest the news. He said, "It takes more than grades,
especially for you. It's time for you to start praying. You alone
cannot make it happen."

FAMILY TALE 19

Tell me you recognize me
The mirror
calls me forth
with new eyes

I took the priest's advice and tried to attend mass every day. It was hard. I looked at girls at the church more than what was happening on the altar.

No matter what happened, my grades had to improve. It was my ticket to freedom. I needed help. I could not go to the priest, afraid that he would send me to confession or to do more prayers.

The bookseller found me coming to his store early one day.
"Nothing better to do today?" he asked.
"Something is bothering me," I answered.

I told him the bad things I did, stealing from my grandfather's pocket and cursing Mr. Wong to his coffin. How these two bad deeds might doom me from going to America.

He did not comment. All he said was, "Come and give me a hand to clean the store front."

The next few times I went to the bookstore, he gave me chores to do. At the end of the month, he gave me a hundred dollars. I was shocked. "Why?"

"It is for you to know you that you can make your own way in the world."

"I do not know what to say."

"What will you do with the money?"

"Spend it on something?"

"Wrong. Keep it in your wallet always. Then you are never without money."

I did not see the logic and asked tentatively, "I can decide what to do with the money, right?"

"Of course," he smiled, "a good person has a generous heart. I hope one day you will know when to invest in a worthwhile cause."

Family Tale 20

I need to know
more than ever
what lies ahead.

I received my acceptance letter from a small college in Kansas. I was elated.

Grandmother bought me a suit for my travel. I wore it to a cousin's wedding. I arrived late. The banquet hall was full. I saw my aunt and went to sit by her side, To my surprise, on the other side of me was the fortune teller. I was about to walk away to find another seat.

She stopped me and said, "I heard that you are going away to America. Let me do a reading for you."

I was going to object. My aunt leaned over and said, "Let's hear it. What can you see in his future?"

She cleared a space on the table and threw the coins.

"You have a special gift."

"No kidding."

She was serious, "Do not become food for the spirit realm."

I answered, "I am just a student. Occult power is not what I am after."

"Still, the temptation is great."

She looked around the room, and then said, "You are a student of life who will become a teacher of life one day. Your path has already been chosen."

My aunt overheard and laughed, "How much does a teacher of life get paid?"

Family Tale 21

I am on my way
to a new way
of relating
among all things

The day before I left home, I said goodbye to the city.

I went to the bookseller. He gave me a copy of Shang dynasty oracles, "One day you will find this useful."

The priest gave me a rosary, "Don't forget to pray. What you cannot do by yourself, with God's help you can."

I dropped by to see Mr. Lee in the Botanical Garden. He gave me a Parker fountain pen, "Keep a journal. Be an observer of life. You may write a book one day."

Finally, I came to my favorite spot by the harbor. I sat in the same spot like I always did for the past few years, watching as life went by.

Nothing I saw that day could curb the excitement within me. In the late afternoon, the wind had moved to another direction. Ferries and boats reluctantly changed their course.

Tomorrow I would board the ship of destiny, my thoughts already ahead, to a land unknown.

FAMILY TALE 22

Listen, listen
to my heart song
Do not forget me
Do not forsake me

August 12.

My day of departure.

My bags were packed, eager for adventure. I was anxious to get to the dock.

Grandmother stood by the elevator, "I am not going to see you off. I don't like good byes.

Go now and be a good boy. Don't forget to write."

Those were her final words to me.

She did not say, "Come back soon."

A small frail woman, forever wise in my mind's eye. I buried her deep inside my heart.

One day, I will return to listen.

Family Tale 23

All we seek
is to break free
from the past.

I left for America on an ocean liner, President Cleveland. I shared a cabin with three other young men my age. We slept on bunk beds. All of us left home for the first time.

After the ship pulled away from the harbor, I stayed on deck, long after everyone had gone down to sleep. I wanted to savor the moment.

I did it. I left home. I was nineteen. I was free.

In the middle of the ocean, darkness brought out light from all the stars. I felt I could reach out and touched them.

I was living a waking dream. I looked back towards Hong Kong one more time and asked my ancestors for their blessings.

My life was spinning out moment to moment, unfolding pages turned by unseen hands.

I sent out a silent prayer, "Guide me on my path always."

PART FOUR

THE EXPLORER

o

o

o

Each step you take

will reveal another

INITIATION

Soft winds guided my dreams into a misty harbor.

I was the first one on deck,
to watch the morning fog roll off the hills.

San Francisco.

My new beginning.

I fell off a cable car
with stars in my eyes.

People laughed.
Someone helped me to my feet.

There was freedom in the sky.

I would know happiness and its many disguises.

A quiet excitement stirred in me
saying "yes" to life.

THE FIRST DAY

The wind was strong.

I stood on a rock,

facing the ocean.

I had finally arrived

to the land of eternal blossoms.

The sounds of laughter

became seagulls,

as evening glow

reached out

to close the day.

The Game of Summer

I learned to play baseball in Kansas one summer.

My first catch was memorable.

I took off running at the sound of the bat.

My eyes could not follow the ball,

but in my mind I could see its path,

arching towards a fixed point in space.

I raced to the meeting place.

At the last moment, I turned to look.

The ball hung in midair,

waiting for me.

I flagged it down into my glove with liquid ease.

The impact filled my body with fire.

The roar from the people watching was like thunder.

I kept on running till my legs gave out.

I was young forever.

Fluorescent Hymn

In Boston Common,

a young man played saxophone,

an instrument older than his years.

His notes were simple.

They held the corners.

From time to time,

a melody burst through

to smooth the edges.

A crowd gathered around him.

I was a stranger in the city.

His music kept me company

as evening poured out its stories.

Hacienda Del Sol

Tucson,
America southwest,
vibrant blue sky
voluminous cloud.

Relentless light blinded my eyes.
As the midday sun pounded shadows into the earth.
A lizard and a field mouse ran into each other,
settling under a shade to chatter.

The heat must have gone to my head.
I thought I smelled cinnamon.

Someone sang into my ears,
a tune from the Mediterranean.

I let myself sink into tall visions
of giant cactus and deep canyons.

Releasing the sadness
that had been ruling my heart,
my spirit unwound
to follow an ancient path.

CHANCE ENCOUNTER

In Angel Fire, New Mexico,
at a conference about angels,
I met a woman
who had walked the plains of Minnesota.
She told me stories of the sisterhood
and others.

She massaged my feet.
They became soft like cotton.
I fell asleep and forgot to meet her in the sauna.

I woke up on a couch
in a hotel lobby.
Three AM
The world was lost in slumber.

I saw her one more time.
She gave me another massage under a tree,
and chanted for me a new dream.

I looked at the clouds,
and saw the many adventures
that would come into my life.

GOD HAS A PLAN FOR EVERYONE

Paris, the Louvre Museum.

In front of a Van Gogh painting,
tears came to my eyes,
for no reason.

Outwardly, nothing happened.
Inside, I was altered.

Later, I stood on Pont Neuf,
a bridge between the Left Bank and the Right Bank,
feeling lost and all alone in the world.
The sun was setting,
a most romantic setting,
but my heart was in desolation.
"Who am I?"
What will I do now?"

Then it happened.
The First Visit I would later call it.
It was as if someone tapped me on my shoulder and whispered,
"You are an artist."

I felt the touch of an angel,
whose hands lifted me
to release its splendor.

Many years later, I realized
it didn't matter how many times I lived to return to Paris.
That day, that moment,
my life changed forever.

BEIJING

I learned Tai Ji in Beijing,

at the east Gate of the Heaven Pavilion.

My teacher, a retired factory worker,

a proud man,

would not accept me as his student

until much later.

But then,

I was not to keep my obligations to him,

as a student of old customs.

I will always remember him fondly,

who taught me old ways

from the Middle Kingdom.

I still practice Tai Ji.

I am now much better.

TAI SHAN

Tallest mountain in eastern China.

Emperors came to make offerings to heaven;
I came with my mother.

The journey up the mountain
was a pilgrimage of redemption,
a ritual older than one could imagine.

At South Heaven Gate,
an old woman in her seventies
walked with her grandson.

I asked, "Why are you laboring up the mountain?"

She answered, "I come once every year for my heart to be healed.
Ahead is someone even older."

At Mid Heaven Gate,
I caught up to the elderly woman
leaning on the arm of her great grandson.
She gave me a toothless smile,
"Up in front is someone you should see."

There she was, the frail form of an old, old woman,
being carried up the trail in a basket
on the back of a carrier.

I saw in her eyes,
stories of a hundred lives.

My mother pulled me aside,
"Let them be.
There is nothing for you there."

I looked around.
We had reached the top of Tai Shan,
the top of the world.

My mother asked, "What are you thinking now?"

"That one mountain is like another."

We sat down and talked,
sharing stories of travels and faraway places.
I made her laugh with what happened to me
growing up in Hong Kong,
and studying in America.

Her eyes were wet,
my heart was tender.

The evening breeze came and listened.
They took her tears away,
and lifted our hearts beyond the mountain.

It was my only journey with my mother.

My best journey ever.

PART FIVE

THE SEEKER

o

o

o

Can a stone statue

become sentient?

"We are a way for the Cosmos

to know itself."

- Carl Sagan -

ZEN

You may seek

the wisdom

of the world.

I simply want

a garment

that fits me well.

Undiscovered Liberty

My sense of elation barely contained

There it was,

in the distance,

a garden I have not seen before.

A garden I have not yet entered.

I don't have a choice.

I have my path to follow.

THE WAITING

There is a doubt.
Is self realization more important than falling in love?

Before his journey,
the seeker ponders.

There is a landscape
he must discover in solitude,
to come to know himself,
to leave behind his troubles.

There he will face his shadows,
turn on the light,
and watch
how they fall off his shoulders.

THE DREAMING HOUR

Outer space is silent,
inner world is loud.

A single thought
fills the room.

A folded map
covers the journey.

The seeker opens the window.

City lights have chased
the stars out of sight.

Electric dreams
neon shadows

He packs his memories
into a suitcase,
labelled to eternity.

Finally, a way has been found
to fill all the silence.

ASPIRATION

On the edge of wonder

In a temple

in the woods

a bell tolled

My worries

quietly moving

faraway

Quiet whisper

another earth

another sky

My heart is full

Decision

Point me to the right direction

Autumn,

the calls of nature fell silent.

Between lingering thoughts,

the wind came calling.

It belonged to no one.

On the mountain,

lonely prayer wheels spin their magic

connecting songlines from the ancients.

Winged pines carry messages

pointing to future directions.

The calling has been purposefully recast,

to embrace all the mystery

that would follow.

LUMINESCENCE

The Radiance Sutra says,
"Keep it simple."

Parting way with insomnia,
a single candle,
his lone companion,
the seeker asked himself,
"Did I make the right decisions?"

In predawn silence,
the world took on a luminescent contour.
Mythical inventors
turned back the hands of time.

The tree of life
bowed to a modern audience.
Preexisting realites
dissolved into an alluring symmetry.

Every question was answered;
every wrong turn, forgotten.

Perfect light and
imperfect stories
converged to a sigh
of eternity.

What was I expecting?

A campfire wouldn't be as exciting
if it were silent.

Rainy days are intoxicating

to the senses:

hot coffee,

a warm croissant,

moments to ponder

the flow of life -

one act plays

with many curtains.

First Encounter

Full moon
night sky
warm breeze
cinnamon tea
we sit together
thoughts flow
in slow time

The clock ticks
midnight hour
plants reach out to touch me
shadows move aside
by a purer light.

My friend, you're going to fly
as a dream comes to your bedroom door.

A scented presence pins you to your chair.

All the feelings rush into your heart.
The first blossoms
reach for the sky.

THE BREAKTHROUGH

Museum of life

tumbled in the dust

claimed by the forest

faded into time

Form and color

reveal their secrets

the emptying of history

has just begun

Recognition

The enigma of discovering the truth

The fragrance of tea

floating world

dancing dreams

All doors are turned to me

I take the gifts

the seamless matrix of the universe

fills the void

THE MASTER

Satsang one

In your presence,

I found

silence

brimming over

with joy.

You touched my head

and said,

"What a beautiful boy."

MASTER

Satsang Two

I open my mind

to the rising wind,

gathering thoughts

that fell off

the banyan tree.

The master took my hand

and said,

"It is time now

for you to work

in the market place."

Bliss Comes as a Gift

Satsang three

The seeker

sits

in the dark

Silent lotus

on a painted pond

white fire

burning his soul

upside down

BLESSING

Satsang four

When someone is healed

from pain,

a silent prayer

rings through

the night.

In Pure Land,

Amitaba Buddha

turns the golden disc.

BEHIND THE MIRROR

Satsang five

Listen

to the sound

of leaves

falling.

It is not

suffering

but a new life

beginning.

REVELATION

At dawn,

many ancient Buddhas

riding chariots,

making diamonds on water.

PART SIX

WHITE STONE CHRONICLE

o

o

o

Alongside this world there is another.

THE POSSIBILITY OF BEING

Can life ever be easy
Or is love a story untold?

Words that heal a troubled mind

a river that never runs dry

Love like you have never been hurt

and dance to reach the sky

THE BLUE DOOR

Can you hear quiet raindrops in your dreams?

A hand of the ancients

drew a diamond on the wall.

Evening light trembled;

dolphins sang from the ocean floor.

Messengers returned from the four directions,

bringing tales of many dimensions.

Seekers gathered around the white stone,

on which had been painted a blue door.

Eons had passed,

since anyone had tried

to walk through that door.

ASCENSION

Desire so deeply
An intention that drives you to seek perfection.

You touch once more your heart.
Now you can embrace it,
that which you once cried upon,
and struggled to be free of.

You touch once more the earth.
Now you can walk on it,
that which you once called home
and tried so hard to be part of,

You came upon the white stones.
Now you can collect them.
Each stone holds a memory.
Each memory leads to a place.

The rising sun never seemed so brilliant.
The child's smile never seemed so divine.
You have walked a long long way,
and stood naked under the stars.

You have gathered your memories in one breath.
Your tears have turned to jewels.
Eons of earth's experience
has now been distilled into a drop of light.

All the rivers flow back to the sea.
You touch once more the dawn.
It is time now for ascension
to begin.

NAMO AMITABA

Love is a sacred journey,
return to the boundless light.

Sunset comes to spring river,
a child casts a Buddha smile.
From a broken cup,
a drop of light holds still.

I am on my way to the crystal city,
thousand moments shining in flight.
On the edge of the evening,
all lives become a silhouette.
The mystery on both shores
returns to the one in sight.

On the beach, the seeker
making sandcastles
turning.
The child walked up to him and said,
"Are you ready? Are you ready to come with me to the light?"

The seeker turned to find his belongings.
The tide had come in.
All had been washed back to the sea.

He looked around.
The child had already gone into the light.

Gazing into the last glow of the day,
the seeker smiled.
Endless Horizons revealed themselves to him.
For the first time in a long while,
he could draw an easy breath.

THE GOLDEN VISION REAPPEARS

Permission to dream of a better life

Seek only,
where the mountain meets the sky.
I sit,
and watch the sunrise.
Upon the clouds,
angels keep watch,
crystalline thoughts of changing sights and sounds.

You enter my mountain temple,
invisible laughter catching fallen petals.
As I gaze upon your heart's secret meadow,
the golden vision reappears.
Love is a rushing stream of life,
giving birth to a jade garden in the rolling hills.

You can come to my house,
in the shadow of running water.
I serve you tea in the cool shade
We'll share a tale or two
of the distances we traveled.

Yonder lies a field of yellow flowers,
and a pond of the purest spring.
We will catch a glimpse of our reflections.
Crimson stars ascend on the far horizon.

Another day is drawing to a close.
The silence in our hearts knows
We are the beauty
that places the flowers on the hills.

Here I Am

A perfect moment
is not so common in our lives
that it can be ignored.

Evening light sank deep into the shadows.

In the market place,
a modernist's earth angel
made a sculpture in black sand,
looking to lease a new life,
for those who came by to listen.

I circled the town square,
an outsider of whispered promises.
I was part of the wall,
which held the light at the edge of the world.

Inside,
TSN sports, CNN news;
big city noise, casual humor.

Life is folded in halves -
one page records the drama,
the other,
the truth of what really happened.

A threshold had been crossed.
The story had already been told.
And we both knew the title.

Redemption

Do you ever wonder
what is behind locked memory?

Breathe

concentrate

a naked hand draws a line in space.

The light is solid like a rock.

The world is enchanting to a breaking point.

A new moon creeps into the garden.

An irresistible force shakes the blossoms.

Tidal waves of laughter

full explosion of senses

waiting for darkness to falter

and for dawn

to lift the curtains.

Karma

What could I have done differently?

Fire in the crystal
cool flame
burning

Songs from distant stars
deep space
echoing

Call from Central Sun
no escape
no warning

All for the heart
forgetting
remembering

A new leaf of the old self
forever unfolding

Last Song

I am the eye
longing
to see

I am the hand
eager
to touch

I am the heart
learning
to feel

I am the light
nourishing
self

I am the love
embracing
life

I am the voice
reaching out
in silence

I am the breath
rushing back
to sea

I am the soul
forever
free

God is dreaming for us

as love pours

through and through

About the Author

Synn Kune Loh is an exhibiting visual artist, design consultant, and international speaker on the evolution of consciousness.

For over a decade he travelled extensively in Mexico, leading explorations to twenty pyramids, including the special sacred site known as *The Luminerias*. Synn Kune is an active speaker with the Sivananda Yoga Farm in Grass Valley, California.

Born in China, Synn Kune grew up in Hong Kong. He completed a B.A. in Psychology from the University of Bridgeport in the USA, before his graduate study in Cultural Psychology at Queen's University, in Kingston, Ontario. An accomplished painter, he studied experimental art at the Ontario College of Art in Toronto. In addition, Synn Kune holds a Master's Degree in Therapeutic Counselling from the International College of Spiritual and Psychic Science in Montreal, Quebec.

With his wife, Dawn, Synn Kune Loh currently lives in Vancouver, BC, where he paints, writes poetry and conducts transformative workshops.

Author website: www.SynnKuneLoh.com

13077821R00072

Made in the USA
Charleston, SC
15 June 2012